Catherine Ayres

Amazon

Indigo Dreams Publishing

First Edition: Amazon
First published in Great Britain in 2016 by:
Indigo Dreams Publishing
24, Forest Houses
Cookworthy Moor
Halwill
Beaworthy
Devon
EX21 5UU

www.indigodreams.co.uk

Catherine Ayres has asserted her right under the Copyright, Designs and Patents Act 1988 to be identified as the author of this work.
©2016

ISBN 978-1-910834-19-0

British Library Cataloguing in Publication Data. A CIP record for this book can be obtained from the British Library.

This book is sold subject to the condition that it shall not, by way of trade or otherwise, be lent, re-sold, hired out, or otherwise circulated without the author's and publisher's prior consent in any form of binding or cover other than that in which it is published and without a similar condition including this condition being imposed on the subsequent purchaser.

Designed and typeset in Palatino Linotype by Indigo Dreams.
Cover design by Laura Lawson
Printed and bound in Great Britain by 4edge Ltd.

Papers used by Indigo Dreams are recyclable products made from wood grown in sustainable forests following the guidance of the Forest Stewardship Council.

To my family

Acknowledgements

Acknowledgements are due to the editors of the following publications in which some of these poems, or earlier versions of them, appeared: Mslexia, The Moth, Obsessed with Pipework, Under the Radar, Bare Fiction, The Interpreter's House, Diamond Twig: Inspired by Julia, The Fat Damsel, Domestic Cherry, Amaryllis, Clear Poetry, Deseeded, Southlight, Stepaway Magazine, Spontaneity, Poetry Bay, The Very Best of 52 (Nine Arches Press, 2015), My Dear Watson: The Very Elements of Poetry (Beautiful Dragon Press, 2015), Deranged (Pankhearst Press, 2016), The Hippocrates Prize Anthology, 2015, The Hippocrates Prize Anthology 2016, The Elbow Room Prize anthology, 2015. 'Making Love to LINAC' was third in the Hippocrates Prize, 2015; 'To the Lighthouse' was third in the Elbow Room Prize, 2015; 'Leaving at day break' was highly commended in the Manchester Cathedral Poetry Prize, 2015; 'Walking with Bridget' was a finalist in the Mslexia Poetry Prize, 2015; 'Choosing a breast' was highly commended in the Hippocrates Prize, 2016; 'Hymn to the women in Ward 36' was Diamond Twig's Poem of the Month, December 2015. 'Silence' was winner of the Elbow Room Prize 2016. Quotations from Quintus of Smyrna are taken from *The Trojan Epic: Posthomerica* translated and edited by Alan James.

Massive thanks go to Jo Bell, Norman Hadley and all the wonderful people in the 52 poetry group. This book would not have happened without all of them and I wish I could name everyone here! Love and thanks to Marie Lightman for helping me to start writing, to Beth McDonough, Joanne Key, Tom Sastry and Zelda Chappel for keeping me going, and to Jane Burn, for her friendship and support.

Also by Catherine Ayres:

Dark Matter 5 – poems by Catherine Ayres and Steve Urwin, Black Light Engine Room Press, 2015 (in which some of these poems first appeared).

CONTENTS

Amazon   7

I: Something happened at the hospital

RSVP	11
Choosing a breast	12
Silence	13
Hymn to the women in Ward 36	14
How I lost my fear of needles	15
The cancer patient remembers her time as a bat	16
Making love to LINAC	17
A Nasty Little Goodbye Note from the Disappearing Spoons	18
Family photograph	19
How to see a gene mutation	20
Something happened at the hospital	21
Call me strange but	22

II: A love letter from Disappointment

How to get rid of elephants	25
A love letter from Disappointment	26
Patience	27
Turtle	28
My favourite layby	29
Leaving at day break	30
Messages I did not send you from Paris	31
Pine	32
Curlews at night	33
On heartache	34
Remembering love	35
At Rydal Water	36
Limits	37
Walking with Bridget	38

III: Survivor in a photo booth

First Signs	41
Single-breasted	42
Forgetting Rome	43
Scapegoat	44
The Amazon imagines a first date	45
Experiment	46
Survivor in a photo booth	47
Lioness	48
Zoetrope	49
Rider	50
April 30th, 2015. A birthday card to cancer	51
Lunchtime. The industrial estate	52

IV: Lessons from the dispossessed

Christina Rossetti talks to God after an illness	55
How I helped myself escape from a snow globe	56
Clear skies	57
To the Lighthouse	58
Whale song	59
The fish I would like to meet	60
Wild	62
The Amazon addresses the football mums	63
Venus to the Full Moon	64
Driving out of dusk	65
Evensong	66
Ordinary	67
Grace	68
Lessons from the dispossessed	69

Amazon

You'll be an Amazon, he said,
until one breast later
I found out they had two.
And there was no fight,
just a crawl through white space,
needled, not speared,
all my blood shed in a bag.
Yet four years on,
these women rise inside,
watch me thunder in
from the world's edge –
the men gone,
life strange as a plain.
They whisper:
Sister, it's time
to trace the stories on your skin.
Slick our myths across your chest.
Open your wounds. Begin.

I
Something happened at the hospital

RSVP

An hour's wait.
A line of women facing a wall,
surrendered to hope, clutching
envelopes like white flags.
I've shaved under my arms,
chosen clothes that come off easily.
I don't know it yet, but in three weeks' time
I'll never wear this bra again.

We dither about tea. Should we risk the walk?
Sod's Law, my mum keeps saying
and I wonder if she means our place
in the queue, or that she's been here before,
shifting on chairs screwed to the floor,
the leaflet carousel, its encyclopedia
of unthinkables. We settle into unease,
abandon the crossword for T.V.,
watch subtitles ghost the presenter's babble.

A cuckoo clock of doors and we're in.
Without the paper sheet, the bin marked
'Sharps', it could be a budget hotel room,
this flood of nurses my hen-do,
the start of a messy night.

Instead, I sit opposite a man who whispers
'I'm afraid…', leans forward like a
bar-room creep, doodles my curves
on a paper scrap and crosses out the tits.
His picture jellies my ribs, turns my heart
into a fish. My mum grabs his arm, shouts 'Stop!'
Too late. The party's started.

Choosing a breast

She helps me onto the trolley
and we chat about our sons
to distract me from the tug of the drain
in my side, a cunning snake that bites
its way out, leaves an ellipsis, a bloody
'What next?' on the spotless floor.

I'm placid as the pierced Christ,
my eyes following her Crocs to the
cupboard at the far side of the room.
She opens the door to a mortuary of pelts,
spineless hedgehogs in cellophane:
These are softies. Choose a size.
She crackles them open;
it's like Christmas on Mars.
Small? Medium? You're not large.

And of course I ham it up,
hobble out onto the ward,
make the old ladies laugh
with this foam pet in my palm.
Later, curtains closed, I clutch it
to the padded hollow of my breast,
solemn as Nelson in the ward's glow.
It sheds its final prickles in my eyes,
spikes a line across my severed chest.

Silence

The last man to touch my breast held a knife

My lover said nothing;
his eyes told me to wear a vest

Sometimes I spread my hand over the scar
to feel its cage

How does a woman speak
with a closed mouth on her chest?

She unpicks in silence

until the rain comes,
like burst stitches on the glass

Hymn to the women in Ward 36

Under skittish strips of light
we are a line of sallow fools,
panda-eyed with weak tea and waiting.
Our lives crawl round these chairs
like the fat babies we will never have.
Let them suckle skirting; we have no breasts
left, only thin smiles, red lips grazing gauze.
Don't worry, we know it's not alright.
There are no soft dawns in us now,
no platitudes scribbled over peach skies.
Hands off, we're hairless dolls, cocked heads
hooked on the clock hands, looping our veins
through a circle of skipped beats. It is best
to stare out time alone. There are bulbs
in our hearts, my darlings, scales cupping
fresh skin. Soon we will push our crowns through
spreading hands, nod praise to a different sun.
We don't know it yet but these days will writhe
free, fall as quiet as carrier bags kissing concrete.

How I lost my fear of needles

It was all in the wrists – the way
I made one flicker like a leaf as
I opened the other with a butter knife
and watched my fear haemorrhage
into a precariously balanced sieve.
The weight of release tightened my arm,
made it quiver like a washing line.
Time quickened. I rinsed away
the stench of wet wool and piss,
forced my fingers to separate jellied
clots as you force bare feet into a bath
full of beans. I punctured its blackness
and bled it dry, felt a small sharpness –
no more than a red breast in snow –
then the softness of a window veined
with cobwebs, the triumph
of my unclenched fists.

The cancer patient remembers her time as a bat

They sleep through crucifixion,
they are candle wicks, snuffed.
They hang like mouldy clappers,
wear leather blankets, cluck.

They are sopranos, radar stations,
their Mickey ears are mussel shells.
They are black grapes, oozing juicy,
they study the silence of bells.

When I was bald, ears Spocked,
my eyelids rustled with squeaks.
I peeled wings from my heels,
built a belfry in my chest,
chased echoes for twenty four weeks.

Making love to LINAC

Your clinical geishas prepared me for you.
They mapped out my body with indelible ink,
ready for your measured gaze. I waited for them
to bring me to you, stripped in a mirrored cubicle,
struggled into the plain blue gown they said you liked
because it opened easily. I heard them laughing
about last night in another room. Sometimes I cried,
still shocked at my bald head, its too-full moon.
But I accepted our encounters. Even though you made
me sad, you never made me feel unworthy.
Before we could be left alone they pressed my limbs
into moulds, lifted my arms above my head so my breast
was pert again, my scar's clenched fist stretched
smooth, almost beautiful. They squinted at prints
of my contours and read out my co-ordinates like weary
Girl Guides. I felt myself slide under your influence,
unfold into immensity. I rose towards you many times,
a willing sacrifice, watched from behind glass by disinterested
voyeurs. Music played. I saw your inner workings, felt a deep
shudder of rotation as you burst a million cells inside me –
little deaths so I could live. When it was over, I hung my gown
in a plastic bag and walked away. I could have felt empty,
our fractions of time a strange white dream;
but I kept your heaviness in my limbs,
a square of your kisses slowly reddening my chest.

A Nasty Little Goodbye Note from the Disappearing Spoons
or Understanding The Spoon Theory

We'd fed you for too long.
When your bulbous faces first receded
in the backs of our bald heads,
you drank yoghurts,
enjoyed the thrill of squeezing hot teabags,
forked out on cheese knives.
But when the dishes joined us,
a new fear stirred.
You had underestimated our power
to turn the world upside down.
How you searched for us –
chasing our shimmering handles
down dusty roads, thinking you'd seen us,
upturned and luminous in the armpit of a mountain,
only to find it was the disappointment of a loch.
Fools!
At dawn we will tinkle round the milk bottles
for the last time, then melt our silver into the fading moon.
So huddle as close as your noses and knees allow.
You cannot make spoons.
How you will long for soup!

Family photograph
i.m. Florence Taylor

Here's the chromosome, sausaged into an X,
bulging with DNA that spirals like telephone flex
or dead curls on a bathroom floor.

Close up, it's a gymnast's ribbon,
each double strand holding an elegant ellipse,
a chain of sound holes strung with genes.

This is not us.
Our guitars have been smashed,
our mutant genes twang.

We all hold this broken tune:
me, my mother, my grandmother,
all the mothers who came before.

How many were silenced by their breasts
until we three Amazons played on?

How to see a gene mutation

in the crackling dome of suds rising from a plughole
in a line of cats' eyes blinking through fog
in the strange crawl of a wasps' nest
in rain prickling a windscreen
in jackdaws fattening a bare tree,
their black buds sharp against twilight's scars

Something happened at the hospital
or The Amazon experiences scanxiety

The first time I flew to the moon
I was bent half-naked on a bed,
watching the black hole of my stomach
implode against the waistband of my skirt.
As the doctor caterpillared my neck with cold
fingers – her hair falling across the closed eye
of my scar like an extra stitch – I flickered
like a shadow on the ceiling, admired the ridge
of my spine under the strip light's snow.
It's hard to cling to facts when you're flying
through space; the force of possibilities flung me
light-years away, shivering in a circular depression,
a half moon bouncing in a shadow of doubt.
I came back to earth outside the café,
slipped with hypersonic speed through
the crack under the door, eyes dizzy with stars.
The other rookies were waiting for me;
we fumbled for teaspoons with nearly-numb hands,
the atmosphere heavy between us,
mouths caked in dust.

Call me strange but

I don't find breasts amusing
eyelashes in a palm are the bodies of transparent butterflies
I wear the same clothes every day
pulling the skin off the sole of your foot is a form of meditation
I often think about discarded flesh
pink is not the colour of cancer

II
A love letter from Disappointment

How to get rid of elephants

They're fine, doodled in the margins of
hospital letters, so their curves look
pleasingly contained, like shells.

But squeezed into a three-bed semi
they're harder to keep in proportion.

At first it's a bit of a joke. You can
play telephones, whispering secrets
into a tail, while your partner holds
a trunk to his ear, pretending to listen.

And if you lean against one for warmth,
wearing the tracksuit you should have
thrown out after the operation, you can
dissolve into greyness for days.

The bulk of the problem lies in bed,
where a huge flank of indifference can roll
you both, fully clothed, onto opposing
edges, wincing at the sharpness of tusks.

So pick a quiet moment, use their proper
names and ask them to leave. Try:

You Will Never See Me Naked Again
I Want To Disappear
We Still Haven't Talked About What Happened

A love letter from Disappointment

I watch you perform the daily ritual
of routine as if lost in prayer.
Your hands circle a child's face,
fold clean clothes, smooth your skirt
during meetings. Sometimes you look up
to search the clock, the sky;
you are so beautiful when you're waiting.
I allow you moments of anticipation
so I can hide in the flicker of your smile,
hollow out a silence at the end of your plans.
When I come you hold me so gently,
let me wet your eyelashes with kisses
and pull your heart so taut it skitters
like a dying butterfly. When you're alone,
I echo inside you like the memory
of sea in a shell. Don't worry, my love;
I will return to empty you of what you've never had.
I won't fail to disappoint.

Patience

These long afternoons when the trees wear halos and show me their dark sides.

These long afternoons when the birds repeat themselves and don't listen to each other.

These long afternoons when I share the roses with abandoned footballs.

These long afternoons when the cul-de-sac whispers a future of perfect lawns and wheelie bin stickers.

These long afternoons when truth sits on my shoulder and puts its tongue in my ear.

These long afternoons when I know you're not looking.

These long afternoons.

Turtle

It's always like this now:
I have an apathetic heart, turned in on itself
like the hood of a coat in the playground.
A turtle, my son calls it. Yes, I have a turtle heart,
turned in on itself, with a hard shell.
It's peaceful inside and soft.
I love it more than you.

My favourite layby
'Such was Penthesileia fallen from her horse' – Quintus of Smyrna

If you reach the twist of birch you've missed it.
It's just past Robert's farm, where the open door
of the lambing shed is like Christmas in March
and the larch wood weeps into a shiver of puddles.

Stop there in summer if you can.
See the lane fall steeply as a heart's lurch
through the shadow of the fells' high crests.
Listen past the crackle of your cigarette;
curlews will edge silence with a bubbling tide
of sound, the valley soft as a solstice dawn.

Or stop there at midnight, as the year turns
towards storms. Through a squall of hair and tears,
squint at the Plough, ashes scattered in a gaping swell.
Below you a horse will swallow the moon and
tumble into the roar, its sacrifice unmapped.

Leaving at day break

It flew under the wheels
just as morning opened,
feathers snowing through the sun.
For once, I didn't think of stopping;
I swallowed its small death, drove on.
There's a certain light you don't see often,
not the cold, hard kind but a penny-drop
that clicks grey into gold,
the bird you thought you'd killed
arching upwards against the dawn.

Messages I did not send you from Paris

I am sending you this message from the Eiffel Tower.
We are slowly creaking upwards,
seeing blue through every angle.

I am sending you this message from the Seine river cruise.
When we're under a bridge the children scream
and their joy echoes through green darkness.

I am sending you this message from Sacré Coeur.
I am in a cloche full of whispers, staring into the blank face
of Christ. I can't think of anything to pray for.

I am sending you this message from our hotel deathbed.
It's so small I have to spoon myself to sleep.
I can't hear the river twist its thoughts outside your house
or the silence between our words.
I am in a foreign country now.

Pine

This Eden turns my belly
like an unborn child. I feel it kick,
I am heavy with its sweet discomfort.
I'm a woman gone to seed,
overgrown with huge skies.
Dusk velvets my tongue –
I sick stars, babble skeins.
My cheeks bloom winter afternoons;
no pinching reddens their hollow rind.
Bare sycamores stretch my lungs
and the fell spreads like panic in my chest,
its drifted flank a great white horse
that beats lost days into my blood;
they curdle, like a frothing curse.

The rook inside my head
circles a village lost in snow.

Curlews at night

I find a foothold before the huge slab hits,
hoist myself up, foam spurring bare heels.
For a moment, I'm lost in a murmuration of spume,
chalked hands pale through the wave's ghost.
I thread the headland path with careful steps,
a silent speck through the sea's white hiss.
Somehow I hear them, bubbling under
the seagulls' prehistoric shrieks.
Their strange sonar pulls me to another place:
the crackle of moorland brown with sun,
a farmhouse roof that slants in every dream.
I wake thirsty, drenched in salt;
drain their echoes from an empty glass.

On heartache

It's a bell long tolled,
an echo of an echo,
a space that frames an action
and makes it small.
It is close,
a photograph examined;
it is distant,
a road snaked through the fell.
It is a square of sun
on grass once in shadow:
wet-tipped, worm-holed.
It is water sweetened
by surface flickers:
it stretches deep.
It is an old phrase
in new words.
It is every Spring.

Remembering love
'I think about you / in as many ways as rain comes' – Norman MacCaig
'…dreaming you hard, hard…' – Carol Ann Duffy

It comes back slow as fingertips walking up a thigh
under the café's plastic table on a distant afternoon
fat with the promise of thunder.

It comes back silent as the dawn shower we drank
before the lake pressed drops into discs on a mirror
we broke with our bodies.

It comes back soft as the dreich against a window
when my veins were full of static and you held
my head like the sun in your cupped hands.

It comes back hard. Hard as the storm that bit our cheeks
and pulled the tongue out of the fire we built so carefully
in the garden on the wrong side of the fell.

At Rydal Water

There's no name for it,
this soft clank of the past
that presses circles through
a space I can't fill
with ordinary thoughts.
Sometimes it thins into sorrow,
or froths fat as moss
over a sharp edge,
small things singing happy
in the grey of what's left.
Today, there's nothing.
A silent lake.
Water's empty envelopes
at my feet.

Limits

There are things I want to tell you,
like how we went for a walk last night
at ten, striding out past the flickering TVs
to the motorway bridge, as the day held
the memory of itself in a thin strip on the
horizon and you spread slowly inside me
like a bruise. Before we reached the railings
we could hear cars scoring tarmac, the soft
howl of lorries singing of places we would
never see. And I wondered if we should join
them, make love one last time in a spatter
of bones and blood on black and white.
But look at the trees, you said, look how
carefully they hide the tremble of birds in their
shadowed hearts. Does this not give you hope?
I kissed you then, pressing your words against
cold steel, as the night uncurled like a fern frond,
leaving me alone, wrapped in the shroud of a streetlamp,
five minutes from home.

Walking with Bridget
'...in the vast thicket of her grief, she smiles' – medieval graffiti poem, Sigiriya, Sri Lanka

Almost Spring. We left the bridge,
fumbled down the station's bank
and fell like astronauts into afternoon.
We crackled through dead wood,
fly-tip soiling its open grave,
then followed a wake of snowdrops,
a thousand nodding dogs at the railway's
edge, until we reached a copse,
the river's lazy splay, a chance for lunch.
How strange to eat in these margins,
a beak-tilt of sun staining water peach,
the heron's cortège as blue as fells.
You were brushing down crumbs when
I saw it: an isthmus of light sucked between
the trees; a soft anguish, a hidden smir,
which broke in a plume of finches,
fragments smashed against the sky.
And I wanted to say 'I'm empty'
but instead we joked about birds,
how the oystercatchers looked like waiters,
how their neon bills were sharp as scars.

III
Survivor in a photo booth

First Signs

Two cock pheasants are fighting, wings flattened
like the halves of a severed butterfly.
I see the panic of separation
in the brutality of clashing beaks.
The fizzing brown river feels it, too, tries
to reel in its spate with white fingertips,
unable to fathom its fright, folding,
folding itself into a confusion.
Even the swallows' manic scissors don't
slice soft air for joy, but for survival.
My barren body gave birth to this Spring.
I've pulled it from the freshness of my wounds,
left it to weep on the fell. It glistens
like a solemn promise, a consequence.

Single-breasted

Always the echo of what's left,
a heart's empty warehouse
the swim of abandoned light.
We fall through afternoons,
find ourselves face down and framed
in bottom drawers, holding hands
with bastards in a tomb of bras.
The saints have lost patience;
they grant us single magpies,
blow-dry halos, dreams of bad sex.
Night skins us. We drink the street lights'
wallow, lie quivering in an absence of backs.
Try our false dawns for size:
blink through a veil of clean sheets,
suck your finger, spit dust.

Forgetting Rome

If I slit myself open on the sharp edge
of this kitchen sink, I would still taste of you.
Imagine me opening a flank like a wide boy
flashing stolen watches, my flesh spindled
with your studs, their sweet antiseptic.

If I threaded a skewer through my ear and
gouged out my mind's eye, it would weep
solemn weather fronts, your mirage crinkling
in a layby, fizzle out in a prickle of sheep.

If I unravelled my stomach in a frenzy
of chapped fingers, I would find hair haloed
in a hulk of pine, a lace of puddles
in a potholed road, twisted smiles.

I pretend to let go of what we no longer own.

See how still I am, a statue of Our Lady
refusing to weep, a swivel-headed
demon-child the priest cannot purge.

Let the trees burst their veins against these blank afternoons;
I am fattening my blood with our fallen empire.

Scapegoat

'My poor scapegoat, I almost love you' – Seamus Heaney

Everything's fucked, half-mooned with hooves.
I test my lips on these tender flowers
but I'm never not nibbling a knife edge,
squeezing my neck through invisible hands.

She'll be coming down the mountain they jeered,
when I scrambled away like a cloven bike,
ears as flat as handlebars, days rolling
past my ankles, sharp as scree.

No one tells you what to do with all the unfamiliar,
so I eat it, my tail frayed with trying.
Yes, it has come to this. Twist my horns
like taps and suck out the last of the sweet,

I'll bleat you a flat song, thick with sin,
a bearded Alice quivering with curiouser
and curiouser. I cock my head round a fence
to check I still don't matter.

Can you see the coffins in my eyes?
I smell blood on a stone slab,
my mouth a slit throat, smiling.

The Amazon imagines a first date
after Buddy Wakefield

I spent ten years as a full time martyr.
I was aiming for Saint Cul de Sac
but the Pope doesn't canonise kitchen sink crucifixions
so I stopped crossing my heart.
There are too many hiding places in a fixed smile
and nobody found me.
See these moths under my eyes?
That's from not blinking.
Choose your words carefully,
I'm still reading the ones etched on my eyeballs.
Second chances only happen once;
after that, it's like bleeding onto a flag
and organising a bullfight.
This steak knife reminds me of absent flesh.
Forgive me, I don't mean to be brutal.
If disappointment was a lifestyle choice
they'd sell that sinking feeling in Tesco.
I've searched the greeting card section –
With Sympathy doesn't cover it.
Please seduce me out of this flat mood.
Of course I'd like to fuck you but I'm not that easy.
You can't kiss away my scars.
Press your lips against them.
You'll be the first.

Experiment

'A wound gives off its own light...' – Anne Carson, *The Beauty of the Husband.*

I sliced the scar from my chest,
watched its smile fade between finger and thumb.

I proceeded to isolate grief,
pipette its line of power into a tube.

The specimen grew fat,
filmed the glass with sorrow's glow.

Observe my wound weep in a finger of light,
its tinfoil rustle a phenomenon.

Atomic number 49.
Classified as indium.

...when it is bent, indium emits a high-pitched 'cry'; [it] is able to wet glass; it is used in LEDs – Wikipedia.

Survivor in a photo booth

'Even in the dust and blood where she had fallen / Beneath her brows the beauty of her face could be seen / Still undimmed by death' – Quintus of Smyrna

Skin the colour of flies' blood,
blank Sundays, spit.
Hair a dustbowl halo.
Eyes' blue skies snaked
round ink clots, guessed at.
Lips glassed with gloss,
sliming a slug's Mona Lisa.
One face angle-poised, half afraid;
the other eyeless, sly under a jumper's rag,
its scabbed mouth pressed against
a dune of plastic flesh.
Here's the camera flash.
We don't smile.

Lioness

When I was kitten
I had a head full of string.
My starry paws boxed stupid.
I learnt shadows,
frosted fur Mohicans
in swamp-eyed fright.

When I was full feline
I pulled slinky back viaducts
and Dracula yawns.
I was flat roof sun spot
freight train purr.
I ate life sideways.

Now I am nine;
bone-shrunk, mouse-drunk,
shawled in myself.
I sick up white feathers.
The blackbird strikes a snail on stone.
I let him.

Zoetrope

Night bellies
with a universe of wasps,
slips through a seam's itch
into slow mechanics of light:
a spool of film, a departing train
that squares the trees in amber,
traps their nodding crowns.

Silence. Then the first fork splits
in a ploughshare's glint,
unearths a furrow of growls.
So this is rage. I could spread
inside its wound, face myself.
Instead, I flicker between slits,
spit shadows, a painted horse.

Sky's insomnia outstares me;
my feeble curve, the patterns on my skin.

Rider

Dawn bucks like a wild mare, throws the moon into blue,
the glint of stirrup and bit in morning's sharp light,
dust already rising, hooves purple on my chest.
Last night I whipped my life then crawled away, alone.
It always returns, egg-white eyes, its steaming champ
in the kettle's boil. Under a dribble of birds,
the siren's squirming terror and delight, it bleeds
through the horizon's line, the desert in my throat,
makes me swallow it down, fat with thunder and scuffs,
this beast I don't want, this filthy skitter of bone,
rain, traffic, pavement's flank, a broken heart, all horse.

April 30th, 2015. A birthday card to cancer

No one remembers, just the rain
making ribbons of the road,
a mile of black sash between home and work,
blossom's flesh a suicide in pink.
Bastard, it's three years since I birthed you,
since you popped a socket in my breast
and suckled under her poise.
Idiot child, you killed her;
the blame is on your severed head.
So here's a card to say that I remember,
here's the paper cut on my chest.

Lunchtime. The industrial estate.

May smells of hospitals,
everywhere a gossamer of flesh.
Blossom skins the drains,
curves a bright scar on concrete
and the sky's a theatre gown,
a blue swish. I wish I could slip
behind the skip's muddled brain,
cool my cheek on roadkill's plump
and sleep through Spring.
But there's no escape; this hour is up.
I drive away down the backroad's
filthy sleeve, leave the rabbit's breast,
its quiver of flies.

IV
Lessons from the dispossessed

Christina Rossetti talks to God after an illness

How reptilian I become! I draw
these walls around me like slimy depths,
crack open my words before they hatch,
scratch their echoes with palsied claws
until my thick neck twists around silence.
This morning You brought me Summer,
the yellow moon of my head fading into new
light, a cross stitch of shadows and birdsong.
You kiss my eyes with these roses, tapping their
sorry heads against the pane. I will force myself
to swallow their beauty, give thanks for the penance
I have paid, my sallow skin pressed against glass.

Between 1870 and 1872 Christina Rossetti suffered from Graves' disease. She recovered, but her appearance was permanently altered. (Source: The Poetry Foundation)

How I helped myself escape from a snow globe

Unstick me, please, the world's turned plastic.
I'm as feisty as a fingernail, cloched in kitsch.
I can see you gurning, bulbous twin;
stop smearing rainbows across this curve –
tend to your little witch. I'm waving, not drowning,
breath caught so often my lungs have run out.
It's heavy weather, waiting for redemption;
my world is floating in fragments, a wonderland
of white lies. Here's the plan, sunshine: let it snow!
Bring this clown's gavel down in a blaze of light;
we can smash this circus into smithereens.
I want the old life behind me, Technicolor tragic,
an upside down oddity stamped against a wall.
I'll gouge out this glass eye if I can suck up
enough sun. How about a pinhole in the North Pole,
broken stars bleeding in your palm's eclipse?
Let me splash a pompous puddle at your feet.
I want to glitter your soles with glycerine.
We could be wondrous.

Clear skies

'...a peek at the unarmed Amazons relaxing at the seaside reveals a seldom-seen sensual, vulnerable side.' – Adrienne Mayor, *The Amazons – Lives & Legends of Warrior Women Across the Ancient World*

For a long time I hated scorchers,
their blank masks, their stick-on smiles.
I was too bruised for more blue;
his leaving was a wide enough sky.
I wanted a thick stretch of 70s,
dog shit surrendered on tarmac's lech,
an afternoon edged with ice creams,
monkey's blood on a knitted dress.
I wanted seagulls sharp as broken teeth,
monstrous gougers, King-Learing
my squint for a bag of chips.
I wanted back in the small days.
But time took the piss, talked over me
and now it's T shirt weather.
Mine's in tatters; the dark days
bit down hard. I might lie back,
let this warm tongue lick my wounds.
Here's a plane dissecting sky,
broken trails, scars fading.

To the Lighthouse

The curlews mourn through the staiths,
rattle its spine with weeping.
I know their cracked hymnal by heart,
their psalm of hidden tides.
I could swallow this salt edge; I could stay.
But the Tyne, fat slug, writhes on,
thins into slow light. A seagull unfolds,
spreads its wings in a glass shadow.

Whale song

I hear them in the strange dissonance of the fridge,
the hollow roar of the tumble dryer.
On windy days they scatter
high frequencies in scraps of sound,
whistle close harmonies
through a half-closed gate.
I rattle with their repetitions,
a Russian doll layered in lament.
I'm going to sing back an echo.
It will rise like a moon in my throat,
spread through a staccato of doors
and disappear in a lorry's howl.
I will find silence.
A small ache of sunlight.
My shadow flickering like a fin.

The fish I would like to meet

He's butchering a rabbit in the kitchen,
the one the dog brought in from the fell.
It's not his favourite job but he's good
at it, taking quiet pleasure in the deftness
of the blade, the quick separation of sinew
and bone. He puts the meat into a bowl.
Right, he shouts, washing his hands, *which
little people want to help me make burgers?*

He's reading a text from his mother, hiding
the phone under the table. *Thank you, son x*
He smiles, picturing her speckled hands arranging
stems in the vase she keeps for best. His boss
clears her throat. *Sorry*, he says, *miles away*.
Somewhere to his right, the PE teacher sniggers.

He's crossing his legs, cradling a book like
a broken bird. His overcoat is too heavy for the
weather but it makes the bench more bearable.
He can't concentrate on his loneliness in this fresh
spring light. He looks up and sees two swans
pulling silk balloons across the pond.

He's in bed, listening to the soft drumroll
of the boiler clock, thinking about her.
You're too nice, mate, Dave told him over
a pint last Christmas. *Women nowadays,
they like a challenge.* When did kindness
become such a burden? He rolls onto his back.
And where can he find a woman who likes dinosaurs?

He's made it past the painful, awkward stage
and now he's really swimming, head bobbing
for apples, water falling from his back like opened

palms. He wonders if anyone can see him.
The shrieks of gulls and children swirl in a distant
orbit as he dives, disappearing in a flicker of circles,
a small secret in the cool mouth of the sea.

Wild

Don't overthink. Undress.
The lake is quite miraculous,
its small tongues lapping at your feet.
Meet slowly. Sleepwalk into its glass eye.
Ignore the goose bumps orbiting your
thighs. Sink into liquid elephants, ruffled
doves, until your nose shoves through each
wave and you crowd surf bald crowns, dazzled
by their dapples. The water's fresh as apples.
Close your eyes. Light swarms your lids
like fireflies. Feel the ghosts of glaciers rise
and smooth your belly with their spines.
Fear unwinds; arms smear wasp stripes through
black depths of fuzz. A buzzard circles high
above, its mewl a fingertip on glass. Listen
to it pass. Glance at the shore – your clothes
collapsed as if in grief, your handbag
crooked as a thief – then push away its plate.
Return to shimmers, quivering flowers.
Swim into this clean slate.

The Amazon addresses the football mums

'Many there were who prayed that when they returned to their homes/ They might share the bed of a wife as lovely as her.' – Quintus of Smyrna

You watch me orbit the pitch,
gaunt and wind-blown, awkwardly aloof.
You see a new moon, a needy sliver
who clings to the shadow of her breast
like a lover spooned. I get on your tits,
make your nipples buzz smug with my
hidden wink. You wish me adrift
but ladies, I'm no eyelash tickle.
I prey on your floodlit forest,
score a circle round its square of light.
I clasp the night to my chest's quiver,
shoot Venus from a crimson bow.
So draw your husbands close:
they see me. Symmetry won't save you
now they dream of suckling stars.

Venus to the Full Moon

Through night fragile as an ink-blown egg,
you gawp greasy and sly.
Where has the house left to hide?
Dark walls don't want you; your fingers
whiten secrets, split willow into bricks.
You do not speak to the owls;
they shiver in your white noise,
such delicate pavanes dripped in bleach.
I know you see me.
I comfort a frazzle of stars
with a small mercy, a lack of blinks.
I push love through a pinhead's glow.
Fat tide-puller, I wish you a slit,
a loose string shouldering a shadow.
You will wane. I can wait.

Driving out of dusk

The sea's a rolled eye,
its sclera a spoon.
Soon street lights will stitch
orange pockets into spines,
mourn the empty motorway.
So stop the car,
step into this sleight of hand.
Watch beachfront windows turn tiger;
take comfort in the water's quiet death.

Evensong

I want 80s tunes on the radio
I want to dance like I've never been in love
I want to mash potato, whisk gravy
I want grains of geese to spiral into dusk
I want a bus to float past like a ballroom
I want the new moon to be bright
I want to pause by the outside bin
I want a line of trees holding leftover light
I want three bodies in a single bed
I want urgent questions about sharks
I want to kiss the flower of an ear
I want thin arms stretching out like stalks
I want to be as warm as a conker
I want the house to curl me in its palm
I want to hear the owls slide through octaves
I want the soft pillow of a yawn
I want a chocolate biscuit at midnight
I want an insistence of stars
I want a mug of tea on the windowsill;
a patch of misted glass, no tears.

Ordinary

Melt into this. This rainbow layby,
this snapped wrist of birdsong, this lemon light
and grass tip, this ostinato thrumming in a brave heart.
Don't stop. Keep balancing raindrops, keep swallowing
bud throbs, keep spooling veins through a bee's wing,
keep foraging sunsets, eating them raw. Accept it,
this gorgeous, this slow burn of normal. Melt into this.

Grace
after an image by Mrzyk and Moriceau

What is grace
but a willingness to shelter pain,
to let its bud swell over months, years
until it splits the locked knuckles
of your spine, flowers through
bone's parting fingers
into a petal of flesh
and you see others
in veined light,
forgive them.

Lessons from the dispossessed
The smallest things are gifts – Julia Darling

You are fallow and there's peace in it,
like November light barely stretching over a stubbled field.
Warm yourself where you can.

A winter tree must wear its stark geometry against every sky
and suffer the feather of birds in its bare branches.
There will be other summers.

Sometimes you will curve your head round broken glass
and be welcomed by the wholeness of the moon,
or catch the grace of an owl in litter unfolding in a lorry's wake.

These things are gifts. Take them.

Indigo Dreams Publishing Ltd
24, Forest Houses
Cookworthy Moor
Halwill
Beaworthy
Devon
EX21 5UU
www.indigodreams.co.uk